AFLAME

Taylor Leigh Bromante

DEDICATION

to my mother, thank you for feeding me beautiful words
since birth;
my father, for showing me the importance of youth;
and my nana, for teaching me that you can never feel too
much or love too hard.

CONTENTS

1   ORO   1

2   VERDE   14

3   AMBRA   40

4   MORTA   56

5   ROSSA   72

ACKNOWLEDGMENTS

Edited by Monica Potts. Cover art by Uriel Lee.

and so she would proceed
to stare at every corner of her room
mourning for a lost love
her newest ventures
were merely sparks and embers
she longed for her heart to once again
combust in the name of lust and fate
she would not settle for being anything
less than aflame

// fuel and oxidant

ORO

at the closing of a day's life
when i am fatigued and weary
rest becomes an unexpected task for my eyes
yet a task of discovery
my eyes draw unimaginable figures
out of gold and purple waves
while dilation fills my mind with patterns
of squirming thoughts and writhing ways
then to conclude the distortion in a climactic manner
darkness inhabits everything
but the stillness of a small, gleaming light survives
it promises that the next day holds something
my mortal ventures never cease
to reach higher heights and deeper depths
so, i am content to say, i am still working
when i simply, commonly slept

// my working eyes

the greatest show on earth
is not the circus
or the nutcracker
but the way i walk around
laughing and smiling
pretending i have it all
when in reality
i'm a fucking wreck
because i'll never have you
ever again
and you're the only one
i want

// performance

i am infatuated with a couple of hours
i would willingly relive the dark, eerie parts
if it meant that i was promised you,
in front of me,
once more for old time's sake
cracking your knuckles
eyes scanning my surfaces
like uncharted waters
i want to believe i am enough
but once we're broken down
who will jump start our lust once more?
i am terrified
and people are terrified of me
i am infatuated with a couple of hours
i am a monster
because they are in the past

// praeteritum

what if i told you
that my favorite pastime
is gazing at you while you sleep?
what if i told you
that you're the closest specimen to perfect
that i've ever come across?
what if i told you
that when i blanketed your body with mine,
i knew you felt my tears hitting your chest
but ignored them nonetheless?
what if i told you
that you're why my mind is in unsolvable knots?
what if i told you
that you're the reason
for my hundred-year habit
of tearing transparent skin off of my lips
until blood is drawn?
what if i told you
that i can never escape these 'what ifs'
and i think you're the mastermind behind it all?

// first love

i want to explore the edge of our minds together
jump off the highest of cliffs
into the deepest of trenches
simply to find anything
we weren't originally searching for
that could inflate our hearts
and leave us dangling for hours

// adventures

one time,
a sapphire-eyed boy told me
that he liked my definition of paradise.
i proceeded to explain my expertise on the subject
with my chin high,
but secretly wondered if there were other denotations.
what does paradise mean to anyone?
the boy hadn't yet realized
that he was indeed a guinea pig
in the laboratory of my mind
when he strummed my leathery sunburnt lips.
little did i know,
he would help uncover a new and improved paradise.
the character with an animated personality,
who lunges for your hand in polaroids
is not the only source of subjective paradise.
nevertheless, i admit, i have longed for someone's breath
winding into mine, constructing a perfect helix,
even while in the most supreme of paradises.
so you could say i was lost,
but until i am found,
i find it absurdly beautiful
that i can define paradise
as a crowded urban stoplight,
where a hectic night can be gracefully seized
by you.

// trance

i hastily depart once again,
too afraid of scarce attachment
and too attached, still, to a former motif
the particles on my skin ache for your contact again
we're hopeless, i've decided
redundantly entering a tempest of misleading lust
your legacy is falsified affection
my eyes widened because i convinced them, i think,
that you lit up the world
and it seems as though no one can rekindle that fire
but i'm still awake and i brought matches
i just thought i'd let you know

// pedestal

i'll never know why
i failed to be more to you
than pixels on a screen
or 900 thread count cotton sheets
but i do know
that you failed to see the heat in my sky
i may not have been the storm
that struck you,
but i'll be back
more electric than you've ever seen
and that's a promise

// faraway storm

they told me
you weren't punctual
i said
i don't want punctual—
i want manic, messy
and the moon
while you're at it

// warning

i can't help but replay
a string of vibrant moments in my mind—
us on bicycles racing through steady summer heat.
you were ahead of me,
commanding all with your unwavering drive.
i could not shift my eyes off you even if i'd dreamed to.
you charged into the evening's layers,
peeling them back like the pages of a novel,
unconquered by any existing barriers.
the earth welcomed our spontaneity with its heavy song.
i inhaled the leaves, the grass, and the twigs
to achieve acceleration.
a multitude of tree roots
seemed to slyly snatch at our tires,
but we prevailed.
we entered a field of tall, pale-yellow grass
that the sun caressed with tranquility.
the most neatly fashioned path
guided us into the afternoon's abyss
where we would become more human
than we had been in a while.
in those moments, it seemed,
you and i were endless.

// the last of june

in between guitar echoes
and clouds of happy smoke
roaring fights turned into unrivaled hugs.
meandering down streets from a fairytale,
one will find a defective brick house
where chaos once lived in harmony
with youthful splendor.
everything crumbled and broke there,
all the while we were building up
the people we'd eventually become

// bungalow

AFLAME

VERDE

in the tempting stillness of the night
while your knuckles graze over my skin
i'll often kiss the corner of your mouth
where your top lip meets your bottom
so that i can obtain a perfect outline
every last millimeter of your kiss
fit to scale
it's not enough to keep hitting the typical target
that fleshy bullseye that i crave
even when i hate
everything you are
i must procure a portion of it
a millionth of it
a lick of it
just so i can have the sultry privilege
of tasting different rations
perhaps i'm conditioning myself
to cut down on the manic, broken love we share
so it won't sting
when you eventually have the grit
to tell me you're done
pretending you're mine

// tendencies

"i've been writing poems about you"
the words seeped out of my mouth ever so softly
as i straddled him in mismatched lace undergarments
he sacrificed a chuckle—something he didn't do as much
these days
"do they say *good* things?" he asked,
"some of them" i said, lying through my teeth

// confession

send me sweet and short
picturesque messages
in the glistening night
seal them with a kiss
or a symbol you're trying out
for the first time
because your feelings are
as unfamiliar as they are comforting
and you can't stop thinking
about being wrapped up in me
how well i know the dozens of knots in your back
and your most tender troughs
then in the morning
blame your poison
and disorderly conduct
dust it off, scowl with disbelief,
ensure that my heart
doesn't swell, puncture if necessary
i love to watch you
mask your emotions
spinelessly retreat
and lie like a fucking pro
you're always my villain
before i've even shook the hand
of the hero

// slipped

i look at old photos of you
pick out the ones where
the lighting
the timing
your stance
your expression
and all else in time and space
is so precisely flawless
that it suggests you once had compassion
curation has absorbed me
so i begin carving a caricature
in my mind
of a different you
the curator submits to the artist in hopes that
something slight might bring you to life.
like an easel that fits a masterpiece
displaying all my favorite color schemes,
i envision you giving more
taking less
and finally becoming the person
whom i know you once sported
a 5 by 7 or an 8 by 10
i'll take whatever i can get
glossy or matte,
no frame necessary
just you—that's all i require

// sequence

i miss your touch.
never needed a welcome,
but still felt so hauntingly invasive.
you were a child ready for a prize—
constantly eight steps ahead of your own accolades.
nothing ever impressed you.
the night sky was never dark enough,
the rhythm never smooth enough,
until you could catch a high that paralyzed
like open, distorted flesh
or a stare from apricot colored eyes.
intrusion can degrade or heal.
while the sun was awake in my room
you said, instead, let's chase the waning moon.
i never caught your eyes on me,
which is why i'm convinced the sun would've been
a better lover.
never again will i refuse its beams.
i hope it forgives like i've forgiven you.

// capricorn

her qualities spurt like a pale hyacinth
diagonally flowing,
endlessly leaping
out of anticipation
and into manifestation
she is the one they deem 'naive'
though, she fosters hope and light
"dodge their words," i tell her
"your center is hidden,
your purity will not provoke vulnerability—
not today at least."

// <flow> er

one time you told me to be more stoic.
i bit the translucent skin off my lip
to taste coppery blood.
i had been alive for 263 months
and had always been a sucker for feeling my heart throb.
whether it was obsessing over boy bands
or crafting handwritten letters to pen pals,
i ached to feel.
but right then, you made me encounter shame.
i had picked up feelings and bad habits, time after time,
and failed to drop them.
then, as i watched you dodge eye contact
and blot out any active remembrance of me,
i felt reassured by my softness
and sucked the blood even harder.
month 264 will taste even better
and i'll proceed with my histrionic ways,
softer than any satin you've ever touched.

// advice

as humans, we have traveled many lonely roads
seeking refuge, sometimes gambling on the destination
i can almost taste the danger
and that's why the introspection
is the utmost beautifully bothersome
there's the road with all the rickety houses,
the longest trip i've taken by foot,
to escape what i thought was youth's golden hours
there's the one that led me to my own sabotage,
albeit disguised as a utopia
there's the one that always felt 100 steps longer than it
really was
and never failed to slice my skin open
with winds cold as betrayal
there's the one that revealed an unsung atmosphere,
where solitude trumped all else
and acoustic strings hushed my worries
lastly, there's the one that made all the other roads
vanish from my hippocampus
because something, for once,
was waiting for me at the end
and that was you

// trek

"r u mad at me"
you? hell no.
you're golden, boy.
in fact you still dazzle me when you
bitch and whine like a (dare I say it?)—
i think i'll borrow this comparison
from you for a smidge—
like a girl.
your tantrums are your best quality
what an enviable trait, good sir.
stars engulf my vision when i read
the nonsense off your lips
they hiss and bite and demand
though i've emptied the pockets of my heart for you long,
long ago.
am i mad at you? nay.
in fact, five words couldn't even begin to
plunge into my feelings toward you.
they're cellular—bouncing and ubiquitous.
eager as all hell.
no, no, honey, i'm not mad at you,
i'm just waiting.
waiting for you to impale my last bleeding organ
so i can be free from answering questions
that needed to be asked ages ago.

// stupid questions

"no"
hushed the dark
my trenches are not for dwelling.
my skies are not for wishing.
my ink is not for writing.
they've taken too much—
claim they love me,
live for me,
but rest their eyes
at the drawing of my garnet curtains

// used

why is it that
one can lather a wall with new paint
over and over again,
progressing to different hues and tones—
a loud coral or the softest lavender,
and not feel as though they are executing memories
or taking possessions?
why is it that
i cannot
arch my back,
abduct my hip,
flip my hair,
for anyone else…
bite the lip of someone else,
gifting back one centimeter at a time,
or drive my fingers along the scalp
of anyone else,
without feeling like his very own assassin?
after all, he left my captivity ages ago
just like those cellophane thin walls—
i left them painted white.

// covering up

his palms graze against yours
subsiding like delicate scarlet leaves
leaving messages that will never be decoded
at first, it will feel like you're falling into your own heart
as if your bones never knew a time without him
every color will pollute your vision
but he is a twisted dark teal
and it's getting late
try your best to not get caught in his storm
he will pass and you will still be here
the world will go on and so must you
grow into your land legs
become your own embellished individual
redecorate yourself as you please
kiss your thoughts every day
for he is temporary, always in a hurry
and you have many other colors to meet

// lesson on lust

once
you jolted your stance
turned to face me
and kissed me
we were on bikes
at a crowded suburban intersection
standing tall like warriors over their steeds
so before i could even respond,
with the rise of my cheek or a murmur
i wondered
if someone was watching
from their car window
to witness
you and i
for once
taking place

// the impossible

when you and her came to an end
and you and i began
i remember staring at you
my eyes plastered to everything your soul had to offer
i wanted to dance in your flames
i remember what you were wearing that one day
a perfectly smart vintage denim button up
i held you tight and smiled so wide
as you told me "i like you. a lot."
you told me how you needed to be her friend
for just a little bit longer
that it was nothing serious
because you "think she's still in love with me."
and i thought that was sweet
until not too far down the road
i realized that i was being dragged through the mud
just as she probably once was—
hopelessly in love with someone
who could never love me how i needed him to
the sky's aura would change and i would
feel you drifting farther away from me
your flames became weak and dim
then i thought to myself—
maybe you were telling them
that you needed to stay my friend
for just a little bit longer
or play pretend that you loved me
for just a little bit longer
or maybe you wanted to use me
for a little bit longer
because you "think I'm still in love with you."
well my dear, i'll save the next girl a few words
just put the fire out
and leave her dancing in the dark

// arson

the last time i sat on this bed
plucking at puffy plaid squares
i tried to right all your wrongs for you
tried to give you the bait
give you something to work with
my frigid hands scooped up my lace dress
to assist you in wiping off the hideous persona
you'd been sporting for the last 14 months
i sobbed while you twiddled your thumbs
thursday's essence will never be the same
my parents' house grows colder and more decrepit
as my eyes scan the floorboards
season after season, the wood becomes a darker shade
acorns fall to the ground,
never kissing their branches again
the tiles have forgotten the tone of your voice,
even though they had once received glossy echoes
as perfect carbon copies
my sleep cycle hasn't been the same since
where there used to be rambunctiousness,
there is now silence thick as soil,
beyond an imaginable threshold
i no longer expect your return
so i will sink my roots
and lift myself out of the kitchen skylight
to see the sun again

// inhabit

since you left
i've been everyone's girl
for a night
for a weekend
for a month
as if i'm programmed—
a systematic rotation.
onto the next one
who may or may not
want me for their phony forever.
your hands turned into his
your lips turned into theirs
your bite turned into
half -assed teething
that knows no passion,
but your whispers i've not found
leaving the mouths of any others.
tell me baby,
what was it you said that one time?
"i want to drink your nectar"
somehow that proclamation stings
like gin in my throat
but also fortifies my youthfulness.
i hope you don't mind sharing with others
because i'm being passed around the table.

// on the menu

do you ever find yourself wanting
to travel back to a time and place
where you were once also wanting
to travel back to a different time and place?
desire is much too cross
indulging in dreams of things
we do not have or once possessed
finding vacancy anywhere and everywhere
perhaps they call it the present 'tense'
because the opportunity of now
creates tension between the human heart and mind
the mind rolls its eyes waiting, ready to conquer,
while the heart bites its fingernails
with a fear of forgetting

// battle

dark, walnutty eyebrows
glooming over glossy hazel eyes
i feel your aching
know your whimper
signals say help, weakness is living over here
but i know your steady, rugged nature
as my own weaponry
it's as if you're wrapped around me,
your diction comforting my insecurities
like an appointed cocoon
you are sunday in human form
father by my side
mother in my bones
warrior on the field
all in one
you have confirmed kills with a glance
but you've taken ammo deep within
the levels of your soul
i need you
i am you
i breathe your breath

// queen

i poured my heart out
over hibiscus and marigold petals
soaked the concoction 'til it bled
steeped until potency fumed
and still he
drank it down
to the last drop
quenching, demanding
never learning to savor

// parched

forgetting
is just being lazy
with handling
all my words,
all my tears,
all our moments,
in confetti form
i nestled them in a tiny box
locked it tightly
and entrusted them to you
did you misplace it?
or did you dispose of it?
i must know

// gift

in our youngest year
you told me you liked the crystals i painted
not 'til then had you even once acknowledged
my artistic ability
let alone my ability to do anything
but sparkle in the confines of your focus
i was too preoccupied
boasting about you to the world
and picking your brain
to hang paintings in my desolate gallery
i had gone off on a voyage
in your cerebral cortex
skipping down the hallways of your frontal lobe
only to abruptly find
your biggest tormentor
i hurried my way out
and returned from my trip, flustered,
eager to pull at your sleeve
like a benign child
telling you what i had found:
a dark silhouette that would never learn
to comfortably compliment anyone—
even the person it belonged to

// self-inflicted

today is your birthday
and although you forgot mine this year
i couldn't forget the frequency at which you blink
over those cocoa colored eyes
even if i tried to
i won't forget your unfailing argumentative nature
or that funny thing you said to the barista
or even what you were wearing
when you undressed me for the first time
meanwhile, you're forgetting
more and more of me each day,
a defect of yours i will always envy

// detail-oriented

nightfall has brought me such trouble
but not enough revelations
when he told me
his favorite thing about my body
was the valley he visited
after overcoming
the almighty walls of
my hip bones
i fell into a trance
now i think to myself,
the valley of empty space
between him and i
on a night like tonight
is much vaster;
it is haunting
and surreptitious
without needing to take
my clothes off

// juxtapose

we spent
3 winters together
3 springs
3 summers
2 falls
all of which my heart was
never in an optimal state.
i forgot how it felt to be
a participant in a holistic love.
i replayed songs 'til my eardrums wept
and shut out warmth
from all sources.
as my idols tearfully sing to the masses,
i'm through with standing in line for love,
waiting for permission,
and hoping that this could be easy.
here's to a new year
with none of you
and all of me.

// good riddance

AFLAME

AMBRA

amber and vetiver
otherwise known as him and i
something new for a change
a bond that was strictly static
it never evolved or flourished
and couldn't sustain
through early January winds
it lured me, but didn't ground me.
all we knew was how to melt
into each other
avoiding the world outside
our cozy fictional globe
he would slave away
lathering my senses,
enchanting my thoughts
yet always failing to keep me
from wandering into the arms of others
still, my receptors remain devoted
to his memory.

// trigger

the slightest moments
that illustrate pages of
you and me
are the most strenuous to forget
despite their simplicity,
their tenancy is rooted
in the coves of my mind
us, discussing comedians
over curry and papaya salad
i'd put my foot up on your corduroys
underneath the dinner table
you would nestle it
and run your fingers up my ankle
without breaking eye contact
or releasing a smirk
you received my trials so gracefully
sparking a love for minimalism
inside of me
that still lives and laughs
from time to time

// stupid, small and frequent

nuzzle your head into my collarbone
as if you're burying
every last ounce of your vanity
and every last fear
of belonging
to a being who feels your thrills
like her own bruises and blemishes
we'll look up
from the dusty ground
and watch the stars dance
coyly leading us
into the journey
of our dreams

// become

often times i'll think about
the nights you used to
slip me on like a silk gown
and trace my curves
like a sketch
that meets perfection
for the very first time,
granting the artist
a little more time indulging
and a little less time drafting.
practice and precision are key
but the creases in your palms
have always known my silhouette
like a childhood home.
the studio has become quite sullen
since you've run away.

// familiar

i got a little too comfortable
with having love
dangled right in front
of my face
you got a little too good
at showing up uninvited
though still expecting
a warm embrace

// obedient

spring is making its grand entrance
you can tell by the smell of composure in the sky
the feel of peace resting upon your face
there's an innate desire to walk outside
for the sole purpose of staring out
into the ocean of earth's air
seasons will always bring truth to centre stage
a transition we've known our whole lives
though not nearly comparable to spring
something about it precedes the most forgiving hours
i'll never forget that spring i captured your gaze for good
dancing in your focus like an open flame
showing you the most underrated parts of nightfall
we drove through wounded back roads
testing my speakers, learning to appreciate
our senses during the hours they typically rest
spring enchants its guests with no restraint
cradles the agony of yesterday
there is no longer cold to taunt you
no more frost to leave you shaking
just the song of the trees
and the stories that rest in their branches
love, it insists,
as if you've never met this motherly season
outside the boundaries of your daydreams

// await

kiss my feet
not because i'm of royal blood
nor because i
have the power to
even remotely harm you
but so that every inch of my skin's
grateful, untroubled canvas
blushes at the precision and
never forgets the devotion
of your contact

// coverage

if he doesn't
stay under
chalky white sheets
with you
'til the morning
has kissed
the afternoon
his heedless nature
cradled in your apprehension
lips smudging
on the sultry skins of
olive toned
freckle-splashed shoulders
then you shall keep him close
for you've dodged a monster
who's soul is bleak
and who only seems at peace
when he sleeps
you've dodged a monster
and found man

// night terror

pull my sleeves up over my head
releasing my flaws
like emperor moths
fluttering to the nearest light
ask if i am listening
to the activities of
our dearest after hours
my sweet, i've been listening
even before you started humming
the rise of the chorus

// unveil

your breathing
emits sounds of
hesitance
dusted
with quiet hopes
i hear you loud and clear
but hear me when i say
i'm here to heal you
and show you that
the best refuge
is hidden
in love

// let me

contemplation
hits the ripples
on the surface of my bathwater
while thursday night
takes its infamously
daunting course
once again
this cold, timid house
begs for a blanket
of warmth and light
that i cannot always
successfully orchestrate
my lips are bruised
not from another
but only thanks to
my own
unforgiving bite
the skin is uneven and jagged
but the water sits on them
quite gracefully
allowing me to become
a river goddess
whose thoughts are
enchanted by spells
and sunken things
instead of sunken hopes
and forlorn calculations
still—i sit in my steam drenched cove
pulling my knees into my slow heart
ready to rid myself of worry,
consume peace
and establish a truce with my mind

// soak

tell me
how can a human heart
beat at 60 beats per minute
when there's so much more
i have to share with you
under the covers, hours before dawn
exchanging breaths that sound
like faraway tides
when i'm tangled up in you
my heart must beat no less
than 300 beats per minute
along with a dozen reasons why i love you
hidden between each one

// pillow talk

what ever happened
to the era of
sinking deep into
the caverns of
his corneas
when balmy, glazed skin
was convincing enough
to delay the days
like honey dripping onto
ripened pears
my only wish in this world
is for it to all slow down
every once in a while

// solstice

the words i needed most
were the ones you never said
maybe in another life
you'll speak up
and i won't be left here with
sleepy lips
an exhausted mind
and a tired heart

// fatal fatigue

AFLAME

MORTA

spring will write songs for you
garnished with precise acoustic strums
fall will call at your darkest hours
and won't stop at anything to find your missing heart
winter will travel far just to
watch you dance with eyes closed
but you will return to summer, beguiled
though his chaotic disposition
has ruined you time and time again

// folly

you used to stare into my eyes
as if you wanted
to submerge yourself in them
like secluded hot springs
inviting a rare
incomparable bliss
why did you come up for air
after drowning in them
for so long

// capsize

a year can turn
dreams and dreaded things
into a vicious reality
it can turn
your prospects into politics
your days into eons
and love into trickery.
while the world warms,
my soul freezes,
but this time
you're not here
to melt me

// cryophobia

i didn't ask you to tangle yourself in my sheets
night after night
or to kiss my spine in a vertical fashion
you're trouble and i know it
a queen disguised as a pawn
you murmur about my youthful ways
and talk a big game
"mischievous girl...
prancing around, turning heads"
you thought i had morbid intentions
but i prefer to lick wounds
so, imagine how useful i felt
when tears began to soften your scruff
i kissed them and cradled your heavy skull
thick knots of dough disabled your throat
you told me
how they kicked your front door down
dragged your dad out of bed
and didn't offer him a change of clothes
complacent with the dark void they had left
i didn't ask you to tell me this story
or to explain to me why you always need
another round even at last call
liquid immunity is what they should call it
i won't ask you to explain why you push me off edges
or why you play with matches and kerosene
but i will ask you just this once
to not apologize
for letting your tears fall
and letting me in

// guarded

hold that tray steady
don't be too this or too that
now clean up the mess

// waitressing

when a boy tells you
you're being selfish
for wanting your 'me time'
tell him
that the organic beauty
and amicable demeanor,
he so longingly craves
in a woman,
doesn't always rely
on the presence
of a man

// self-care

when your eyes lock with mine
my stomach drops 1,000 feet
my soul burns, the ashes linger
do you still think about me?
do you feel the void
weighing heavy on your late nights?
do you have anything left to say,
even if it's just another farewell?
because i have volumes to speak
i disposed of the handmade journal you once gifted me
but continue to write my thoughts down for you
i send them off
to an ocean
of people who hate what you've done
but have never met you

// voodoo doll

i've bitten my tongue
over and over
to keep myself from telling you
how you ruined me
to the fullest extent
never did i know
a human soul
could decay like this
but if i ever got the chance
i'd just be
telling you what
you already know
so instead i'll tell you what
everyone else says—
that i dodged a bullet
and that you, exiting my life,
was the greatest gift
you could've ever given me

// insight

my complacency with being
essentially immobile
in the sinkhole
known as your
relentless, storm ridden world
gave me a permanent residence
with no warm welcome
and a community
of faceless names
who'd never ask me to stay
even if i eventually
broke free

// entrenched

i have a knack for thinking about
stupid things late at night
like when you used to walk me
to my car each night
and how i sat on your lap
in my red vintage chair,
anchored in your gaze
and you in mine
it's funny to think that one day
i could forget all of these moments
it's even funnier that
i haven't already done so

// stupid, small and frequent pt.2

it would be much too easy
and far too logical
to write off the weather
of the past
i'll always be the girl
who chases the storms
of yesterday

// forecast

we both know
the secrets i've had to keep
in order to protect
your intoxicating, untouched life
are much more heavy
than the nonexistent
guilt-flooded reflections
that interrupt your shallow thoughts
i must've forgotten
that men are golden,
never faulty, and
always permissible

// confidant

variety is the spice of life
a recent sermon sourced from my lips
how comical of me to insist
as i've been replaying the same five songs
for years now
in hopes they would
bring me back to that same place
where love lived credulously

// hypocrite

she likes tilted blues
and gloomy greens
analyzing films
and provocative dreams
she rubs her eyes until she sees stars
and has known for too long
that young love's just a farce

// taurean

AFLAME

ROSSA

if i could depict today in color
it would be iridescent
from a classic bird's eye view
eight shades of electric blue
entwined with violet
emerald and orchid
like the scales of me and you
we'll rove into another hemisphere
our souls soaring through pigment and youth

// awake

i've been waiting
for a song
so effortless to sing
the hooks and the harmonies
slip out of my mouth
unapologetically
off they go
filling up my hallways
tilting frame after frame
sneaking into his most
serene notions
and tantalizing his senses
yet always returning
and reciprocating the favor

// earworm

i'll arrange the stars for you
they'll engage in a perfect sequence
combatting the darkness
the two of us
will match our weaponry
in accordance
we agree with ease
to duel in the name
of love and ardor

// on guard

take me captive
to the most otherworldly world
where the sand runs through my veins
the laughter sizzles on my taste buds
and the music doesn't retreat
even hours after
the cynics will sink
into their deepest sleep

// viva

the sun hasn't paid
a fruitful visit
in eons
we've wept together
reminiscent of
steadier moments
swollen with charm
an old friend sits on rusted stairs
fingertips tickling a guitar
as i wait to plaster
the peppered ground
with barefoot splotches

// paramount

mother stands
we rest
she is humble majesty
sunbeams found her first

// provider

streams of saltwater
congeal on my face
suddenly i feel
your gaze drape over me
your own tears landing
on my windshield
you were a quiet, beautiful crier
but you loved loudly
with no remorse
and i'll never blame you for that

// rimani d'oro

my days once knew
this secret, temporary man
he used to tell me i was "a blue"
sultry and generous —
always allowing the world
to rest its head on my shoulder
'til my back would break,
bones mimicking dull blades —
polluted with desolation,
he compared me to the ocean
but overlooked the tidal waves

// pathos

the archeress moves
leaves bound to her hair, plum eyes
tethered to none but the sun

// sagittarius

my, how wrong i was
always putting them on pedestals
only to later find someone
who'd make it easier than ever
to feel both happy and loved
in each inkblot of time

// pinnacle

feeling any feeling
could never compare
to how it feels
being yours
out loud

// showcase

the gardener's glove
will immerse herself
in the underground
rotted roots, earthworms and all,
to invite growth
beyond the sultry soil
a display
which will not stop
at receiving acceptance
from neighbors nor men
it fills the lungs of
women who dig
for themselves and only themselves

// green thumb

citrine skin binding suspicions
those who surrender, once laughed at the hissin'
rampant they sing, but regret they will feel
when her relentless spell
becomes all too real

// transcendence

cigarette ashes danced past
your leathery, caramel colored ears.
our afternoons and evenings
lasted and lasted, defeating monotony—
an eternal novel
with heroes and escapades
all burrowed within suburban walls.
your words became cinematic
to every listener in the room
and myself, your lucky lead role.
some laughs can be felt
traveling every route of one's being—
this was your endless gift to me

// forever

if there was such a thing
as a cunning grimace,
it belonged to you
with flour smudged on your face,
hat backwards,
wisps of hair departing
in every direction,
a face that says "fuck off"
in a million different dialects.
you surprised me with your softness –
a first impression
never could overshadow
the intrepid soul
i grew to know
as my best friend
and timeless ally

// gemini

doodling has always
kept my hands busy
at times i've felt that
ruining everything
has done the same
beneath my quirks
there lives grace
smoothed across
these pages
i hope you've had a good read

// legacy

some say to heal
you must forget
for what is a girl to do
when her flashbacks feud with growth?
to that i say
let's burn them
and unwind in the heat
i'm giving myself the warmth
that they could never provide anyway

// swelter

and so i conquered
this dark, grisly plummet
which took my body
down at record speeds
i was certain i'd yield to a former remedy,
an ugly one, too temporary,
that would land me upright again,
feeling false power and sexuality.
the heat rose inside of me,
an innovator with a heart of ideas
i found my whole self,
resisting and creating,
talking her through the hurt
i am once again, aflame

// end

AFLAME

ABOUT THE AUTHOR

Taylor Leigh Bromante, born May 15, 1994, is an American poet and writer currently residing in Baltimore, MD. Taylor chose to pursue her love for writing because she deeply values the freedom to voice thought and create unforgettable stories. *Aflame* is a collection of unguarded words illustrating the author's voyage to understand love and her role in the world throughout the transformative years of womanhood. As she discovers bliss and purpose, she is also faced with the ugliness and ambiguity hidden within modern relationships. Written over the span of nine years, *Aflame* concentrates on love, loss, family, friends, idols, feminism, depression, healing, self-care, and more. Taylor enkindles a nostalgic and honest energy—often addressing her past experiences and loved ones directly. She aims to sculpt her rawest emotions into elegant writing, while making her readers feel understood and loved.